The Christmas Coin

Jon Magnuson

NEW HARBOR PRESS

RAPID CITY, SD

Magnuson/New Harbor Press
1601 Mt. Rushmore Rd, Ste 3288
Rapid City, SD 57701
www.NewHarborPress.com

Ordering Information:
Quantity sales. Special discounts are available on quantity purchases by corporations, associations, and others. For details,
contact the "Special Sales Department" at the address above.

The Christmas Coin/Jon Magnuson. -- 1st ed.
ISBN 978-1-63357-500-4

For my grandchildren,
Rhys, Micah, Caleb, and Leanna
Because of you, I am truly a rich man.

Contents

Acknowledgments

THE CHRISTMAS CAROLS MENTIONED by title and/or lyrics in this story—

"Christmas Is Coming, the Goose Is Getting Fat" (1885 or 1886, author unknown),

"O Little Town of Bethlehem" (1868, Phillips Brooks),

"It Came Upon the Midnight Clear" (1849, Edmund Sears),

"Joy to the World" (1719, Isaac Watts), and

"Silent Night" (1818, Joseph Mohr)

—are all in the public domain. To their authors, known and unknown, and although long departed from this Earth, I owe a debt of gratitude.

The red, spiral-bound coin book mentioned in this story is, of course, the well-known *A Guide Book of United States Coins*, popularly known as *The Red Book*. My copy is identified as follows:

R.S. Yeoman, Jeff Garrett, Senior Editor, *A Guide Book of United States Coins 2024, 77th Edition* (1974 Chandalar Drive, Suite D, Pelham, AL: Whitman Publishing, LLC, 2023)

I gratefully acknowledge that much of what I know about U.S. coins is a result of reading this essential volume. I was careful, however, not to plagiarize this book in any way. The coin dealer in my story, Mr. Weinman, uses his own words in telling the history of the humble penny. Furthermore, anyone with enough time on his hands to compare the prices of coins listed in *The Red Book* with the values of those same coins as given in my story will note that, although relatively similar, enough to be believable, they are not identical.

I extend many thanks to Brendan Carnes of *Bloomingdale Rare Coins and Gold* of Valrico, Florida, for his invaluable insights concerning the workings and management of a coin shop and the buying and selling of rare coins. Brendan, your expertise is surpassed only by your friendship.

I humbly acknowledge that I would have no ability to write a story such as *The Christmas*

Coin without the grace afforded me by my Abba Father and His indwelling Holy Spirit. May Jesus be glorified in the reading of these pages.

CHAPTER 1

Nick and Grampa Nicholas

NICK HELD THE COIN in his left hand and the magnifying glass in his right. He squinted into the lens as he brought the coin's details into focus. Abraham Lincoln gazed grimly into the distance, no doubt (as Nick had convinced himself) surveying the devastation of the latest Civil War battle. Down and to the right of Lincoln's resolute face, Nick could clearly make out the date—1955. Directly beneath the date, the letter "*D*" now under magnification stood out sharply. Nick knew the mintmark "*D*" indicated that the coin had been produced at the Denver Mint, just as an "*S*" represented the San Francisco Mint, and most commonly, no mintmark at all meant that the coin had been struck in Philadelphia.

With a firm press of Nick's thumbs, the coin popped into the round hole (labeled "*1955-D*") of the blue cardboard Lincoln cent folder. It was the last of ten old wheat pennies that Nick's father had found inside a little box in the back of a dresser drawer and had given to him to add to his coin booklet. Nick leaned back in satisfaction. The empty spaces didn't dominate the pages quite as much as they had before.

"Well, it's starting to look like a pretty nice collection."

Nick jumped at the voice. He hadn't heard his father walk up behind him.

"Sorry. I didn't mean to startle you." Mr. Benson gave his son's shoulders an affectionate shake and tousled his sandy-brown hair.

"It's okay, Dad. I guess I was just really concentrating on getting these pennies into the right spots." Nick twisted in the chair to face his father, his hazel eyes shining brightly. "Oh, and thanks, Dad! My collection *does* look better, doesn't it?"

Mr. Benson patted Nick's shoulder in response and settled himself in the adjacent chair. "Hey, Nick, I just heard from your grampa. He's going to be able to come over tomorrow for dinner."

"Yes!" The exclamation arose naturally and unbidden from Nick's lips. He had not seen his grandfather in a few days and was already experiencing the pangs of absence.

Nick was glad that he had been named after his grandfather but was secretly relieved that their last names differed. Nick's last name was Benson, but his Grampa Nicholas was his mother's father, and his last name was Saint. *That's right*, thought Nick. *Nicholas Saint!* (Or, as he had often printed his name on official forms that required the last name first and first name last, *Saint Nicholas*.)

Nick knew the often-recited story well. It had long been a tradition in the Saint family to name baby boys after actual saints. His grampa's father, Augustine Saint, whom everyone had called Augie, had been named after St. Augustine, and Augie's father, Bonny Saint, was named in honor of St. Bonaventure. When Augie's baby boy had arrived on the scene, his little, round, red face reminded his parents of the famous elf in Clement C. Moore's poem, and so, appropriately, he was christened Nicholas.

Early on, the name caused a fair amount of teasing and embarrassment, but later in life it proved almost prophetic. For Grampa Nicholas was a short man, and although definitely not fat, his stocky stature made him a prime candidate for playing Santa. Furthermore, his hair had turned prematurely white, thinning on the top of his head. "So," he often proclaimed, "to make up for the lack of hair on top, I decided to grow some whiskers. Hiding as much of my face as possible makes me look better anyway!" He now sported a full, white beard, and on those occasions when he played the role of Santa Claus, dressed in red denim overalls, matching checked flannel shirt, black work boots, and a plain, red stocking cap, he made a striking appearance, much more authentic than those traditionally clad Santas so often seen ringing bells on street corners. When thusly attired in public, little children would gaze wide-eyed and wonderingly at him, eventually building up the courage to ask, "Are you *really* Santa?"

Nick's grampa would kneel down and truthfully respond with a very Clausian twinkle in his eyes, "I am indeed Saint Nicholas."

Many children walked away awestruck with repeated backward glances believing they had just met the actual, one-and-only Santa Claus. Nick of course knew better but still felt the same sense of wonder and excitement when in his presence. There truly was something wonderful and magical about Grampa Nicholas, demonstrated in every whimsical smirk, wink of an eye, and strong, warm hug. *He may not really be Santa*, Nick had considered more than once, *but he really is Saint Nicholas!*

And Grampa was coming to dinner tomorrow, and tomorrow was November the sixteenth.

Nick's ninth birthday!

CHAPTER 2

Birthday

THE NEXT DAY WAS a Saturday with (to Nick's delight) no school to interfere with birthday celebrations. At ten o'clock that morning, Nick and his best friend Logan (who had walked over from his house half a block away) hopped in the car, and Mr. Benson, after picking up two more of Nick's classmates, drove them to the bowling alley. (Nick enjoyed bowling even though, as he readily admitted, he wasn't very good at it, and so he had selected the bowling alley as the site for a birthday get-together with a few of his friends. The Bensons bowled perhaps two or three times a year, and Nick was still striving for that elusive one hundred pin game. *Maybe this time*, he thought.)

The four friends bowled two games as Mr. Benson cheered them on with Logan, the most natural athlete of the little group, proving himself the best bowler. Nick, on the other hand, scored a miserable forty-six in the first game. In the second game, however, he managed to roll several spares and a strike, and his score stood at eighty-nine going into the tenth and final frame.

His father stood and leaned close to Nick's ear. "You need eleven pins to hit a hundred. Take your time and see if you can get a strike or a spare."

Nick took his patented three steps to the foul line and released the ball, which headed straight and true (although somewhat slowly and bumping repeatedly on the thumb hole) toward the right side of the front pin. With a satisfying clatter, the pins ricocheted and fell, the final one wobbling drunkenly before it, too, went down.

"Strike!" yelled the three other boys, jumping to their feet, with Nick's father adding, "That makes your score ninety-nine, and you still have two more rolls!"

Well, pepperoni pizza and drinks after the game at the alley's little café area helped to assuage Nick's profound disappointment in rolling two gutter balls to end the game. *Still*, he thought, *ninety-nine is my best score yet.*

Nick and his father returned home after dropping off each of the three young guests, and Nick bounded into the kitchen to find his mother frosting a two-layer cake. "Chocolate cake with peppermint icing?" he questioned eagerly, receiving an affirmative nod. "Thanks, Mom. You're the best!"

With feelings of heart-felt appreciation for the cake and bowling party (not to mention the small pile of wrapped gifts he had spied embellishing the living room coffee table), Nick happily volunteered in setting the table and helping his mother prepare dinner. At his request, spaghetti and meatballs headed the menu, and as Mrs. Benson simmered the marinara sauce loaded with tiny meatballs, Nick got right to work assembling his personal favorite special ingredients—mushrooms, red bell peppers, and onions. These he carefully sliced on a cutting board, then dumped (with an unfortunate splatter) into the sauce.

After wiping the counter and stovetop and mopping the floor, then changing into a clean shirt, it wasn't long before the doorbell rang. The knob rotated, the door swung on its hinges, and, as usual, without waiting for an invitation, Grampa Nicholas strode into the entranceway.

"Hello, hello!" he boomed. "Where's the birthday boy?"

Nick fairly flew to his grandfather and wrapped his arms around his waist, his grampa reciprocating with one arm around Nick's back and the other encircling his neck. They remained in this position unmoving for quite some time.

Nick's parents entered the room. "Hello, Dad," said Mrs. Benson. "Welcome to the party."

"Hi, Lois. Hi, Sam," the elder man responded absently as he dropped to one knee, for he had been distracted by a sniffling sound. He noted the tears welling up in his grandson's eyes, extracted a tissue from his pocket, and handed it to Nick.

"What's wrong?" It sounded like a question, but Nick looked into his grampa's kind face and could tell he already knew the answer.

Nick wiped his eyes and replied, "I miss Gramma."

Grampa Nicholas sighed, and although he forced a smile, his eyes betrayed a lingering

sadness. "You and me both, Nick," he said softly, an arm still wrapped around his grandson's
neck.

As all four of the clan, now gathered at the
entry of the Benson home, were keenly aware,
this was the first birthday celebration without
Gramma Audrey. She had been so full of life at
Nick's eighth birthday party, he now remembered—fun-loving and quick-witted, with her
surprisingly deep and contagious laughter—and
seated next to Grampa with her graying hair and
silver-framed glasses, Nick had been amazed at
how much they really did look like Mr. and Mrs.
Santa Claus.

But shortly thereafter she became sick, and
the doctors said she had cancer. Chemotherapy
caused her to lose her hair, and she wore a scarf
on her head. There were doctor visits and hospital stays, yet she grew weaker and weaker until that horrible day when Nick's mom sat down
with him to let him know that Gramma was
gone.

"She's in heaven now," his mother told him
wiping away a tear. "We should be happy for

her. She loved Jesus, and now she's no longer in pain."

Nick sat glumly. He knew he should agree with his mother, but at present he was more confused than consoled. "Then why do we feel so bad?"

Mrs. Benson smoothed her son's hair. "We feel bad for *ourselves*. We know how much we'll miss her."

Nick thought that was sensible. "Do you think Gramma misses *us* now that she's in heaven?"

"That's actually a good question. I've never really thought about that." She sat in silent reflection for a moment. "You know, Nick, I'll bet she *does* miss us. But time in heaven is different than time on earth. She probably misses us in the same way that you missed your dad when he had to be away for a few days last month. You missed him, but it was okay because you knew you would see him again soon."

The week of the funeral and burial service followed, but as miserable as Nick felt, his sorrow for his grandfather was worse. The vacant, lost look that had replaced the twinkle in Grampa's eyes was almost more than Nick could bear, and so he took it as a personal challenge to get both himself and his grandfather through this difficult time.

As best as he could manage, he wrote Grampa encouraging notes; he persuaded his mother to invite him over for apple pie or coffee cake; but mostly Nick's efforts involved simply spending time with his grandfather without much talking at all.

And happily, it seemed to work. It is said that time heals all wounds. But that is only partly true—time *well-spent* heals all wounds. And as their time spent together wore on, their grief slowly transformed into a warm, unflinching gratitude for having known and loved Gramma Audrey while she had been with them. Nick and his grampa still experienced moments of sadness (as evidenced at their meeting in the entryway), but they were less frequent now and were always followed by the healing balm of fond memories.

"Help me up, Nick," said Grampa Nicholas, pushing firmly on Nick's shoulders and rising to his feet. "You know," he continued, "Gramma wouldn't want us to be sad at a birthday party. She loved parties. This is a time to celebrate!"

"Right you are!" agreed Nick's father. Mrs. Benson took her father's coat and hung it in the closet, and the quartet proceeded into the kitchen.

Dinner soon followed with Grampa Nicholas complimenting the cooks on the excellence of the spaghetti sauce. Afterward, the family migrated to the living room where Nick opened his gifts, and they had just returned to the table for cake and ice cream when Grampa stopped the proceedings to make an announcement.

"I wanted to wait until we were all seated at the table again to give you my gift," he began, addressing Nick. Leaning back in his chair, Grampa reached into his left pants pocket and drew out a small cloth bag, which he handed to his grandson. Nick held the gift in his open palm, scrutinizing it curiously. At three or four inches in length, the bag was surprisingly heavy for its tiny size. The worn, faded cloth betrayed its age, and it was tied at the top both with a somewhat frayed and brownish drawstring and a much newer-looking red ribbon.

Grampa leaned closer to Nick and spoke softly and almost reverently. "My Grampa Bonny gave this bag to me, along with its contents, when I was about your age, Nick. That was nigh on sixty years ago now. I found what it contains to be interesting, but I never really did anything with it, and it's pretty much just been tucked away in a strongbox forgotten for the last fifty years or so. When I realized your ninth birthday was almost here, I thought back to when I was a youngster and remembered getting Grampa Bonny's little bag. Since my grandfather gave it to me when I was about nine, I thought it was only right that I give it to you—you know, sort of keeping the tradition going. I searched for it and finally found it in a closet in that old strongbox, looked it over again for the first time in many, many years, and then tied that red ribbon on it so it would look more like a proper birthday present."

Nick gently tossed the bag up and down and noticed a muffled clinking, jingling sound. "What is it, Grampa?"

"Open it and see!"

Nick pulled the loose ends of the ribbon and happily found that Grampa had tied it in a simple bow (as one might tie a shoelace), and it slipped off easily. The old drawstring was similarly tied, and after pulling its ends and stretching the bag's opening, he turned it upside down over the tabletop and shook it.

A small hoard of coins clattered noisily on the table's hard surface. One rogue copper specimen, apparently emboldened by its sudden release after decades of captivity, quickly broke away, rolling on its rim across the tabletop and over the edge, its escape thwarted by Mr. Benson, who snatched it in midair before it could reach the floor. He handed it to his son.

"Nice catch, Dad!"

Nick looked at the coin he now held, and his eyes narrowed. "I thought this was a penny," he said with obvious perplexity, "but it has a picture of a shield on it, and it just seems too big. And look at the date—eighteen sixty-four!" He flipped the coin over and read, "*TWO CENTS.*"

"Let me see it," said his mother, and the old, copper coin was handed around the table from person to person, each giving it a curious stare.

"I didn't even know there was such a thing as a two-cent coin!" Nick exclaimed. He turned to Grampa Nicholas. "Is it real?"

Grampa chuckled. "You bet it is. And if you look at all of these coins, you'll see that every one of them is from the last half of the nineteenth century. That is, they're all well over a hundred years old." He tapped the two-cent piece that Nick again held. "Just think—when this coin was new, the Civil War was going on, and Abraham Lincoln was president."

Nick's father whistled softly. "Wow! That's a long time ago!"

"Way before my time," Grampa remarked, "and even before my Grampa Bonny's time. I assume he must have collected these when he was a boy or perhaps a young man, and most of them would have already been decades old back in his day."

In his preoccupation with the strange coin, Nick hadn't noticed his mother leave the table, but she now returned carrying the cake, which, after the striking and application of several matchsticks, shimmered from the glow of nine flickering candles. A hearty rendition of "Happy

Birthday to You" followed, and Nick blew out the tiny flames.

Mr. Benson slid his chair away from the table and jumped up. "I'll get the ice cream," he said as he hurried to the freezer.

A happy group sat around that table. Under normal circumstances, Nick would have devoured the chocolate cake with peppermint icing and the vanilla ice cream faster than you could sing the Happy Birthday song, but on this particular occasion, his interest in Grampa's novel gift resulted in many exclamations of astonishment between bites (as well as, unfortunately, a few exclamations *not* between bites) as he simultaneously finished his dessert and examined each coin.

"Look at these pennies, Dad. I thought Abraham Lincoln would be on them, but instead they look like they have pictures of Indians."

Mr. Benson reached across the table, took one of the coins in question, and examined it closely. "That's right, Nick—Indian Head pennies. They were used before the Lincoln pennies came along."

"And check out these big ones! They say, 'ONE DOLLAR,' they're pretty heavy, and they look like they're made of silver."

Grampa nodded. "We always called them 'silver dollars' because they are indeed composed mostly of silver."

"Those are valuable," Mrs. Benson interjected. "You definitely don't want to spend them like you would dollar bills!"

Having finally finished his cake and ice cream, Nick carefully inspected the coins, sorting them into groups. In addition to the pennies, the lone two-cent piece, and the silver dollars, he identified dimes, quarters, and half-dollars, although none of them resembled the coins used today. Instead of presidents, they typically depicted a representation of Liberty, either the face in profile, or on the oldest ones, a full view of a seated Lady Liberty. Nick counted eighteen coins in all.

The grown-ups chatted while clearing the table, but Nick silently stayed seated, gently dropping the coins one by one back into the little bag. With a tug at both ends of the drawstring, the opening tightened, and Nick, following the example of his grandfather, retied it in a simple bow. He rose from his chair, clutching the bag with both hands as though it were treasure. Perhaps it was.

The group made their way to the front door where Grampa retrieved his coat and said his goodbyes. Nick leaned into his grandfather's side, both hands still holding the precious gift. Grandpa Nicholas patted his shoulder affectionately.

"Thanks, Grampa," said Nick. "I really like them."

"You're welcome. And remember, they're not just from me. In a way, they're also from your great-great-grandfather Bonny."

CHAPTER 3

The Coin Shop

"I MADE A DISCOVERY yesterday, Nick. Something I think you might be interested in."

"Really, Grampa? What is it?"

It was the next Saturday after Nick's birthday. He and his mother had made some purchases at the grocery store and were now dropping off a few items for Grampa Nicholas at his home, several miles from the Benson residence. Swiss cheese and pastrami landed in the fridge, and a loaf of rye bread on the counter, before the conversation resumed.

"I was driving home from my dentist appointment, and I thought I'd take a different route home. I turned off Main Street onto Hudson Avenue, and about halfway down the block, I saw a little storefront I'd never noticed before, with a sign above the door that said, 'Weinman's Coin Shop.' Well, I immediately thought of you, so I parked the car and went in. What a fascinating place! All kinds of coins, old and new! I especially noticed a wooden tray on the counter that was filled with wheat pennies to sort through. Anyway, Mister Weinman and I talked for a while. It turns out he had been an accountant in his younger days, but about twenty years ago, he decided instead to follow his dream of owning a coin shop." Grampa gave Nick an impish grin. "I think you would like Mister Weinman, Nick. Have you ever seen pictures of Albert Einstein?"

"Sure, Grampa. He had really wild hair."

"Well, that's Mister Weinman, too! When you look at him, you just think to yourself, '*Now, that's an interesting-looking fellow!*' And he's funny, and very knowledgeable about coins, and he loves to talk."

"I think I'd like to go there and meet him," said Nick with conviction.

"And so you shall! That's the whole point of me telling you all this." Grampa laid both hands on Nick's shoulders and looked at him seriously. "You see, the coins I gave you for your birthday didn't really cost me anything. They had just been lying around in my closet for years and years. So, it seems only right that in light of my discovery yesterday, you and I should take a trip to Weinman's Coins and do a little shopping. Now, if your mother will allow us . . ." Grampa paused, and clasping his hands, he gave his daughter an imploring look.

"When do you want to go?" she asked.

"Well, I was thinking—right now."

Nick clasped his hands in imitation of his grandfather. "Oh, please, Mom?"

She stood silently, arms crossed, eyeing one, then the other, and finally grinned. "Oh, go on, you two!"

"Thanks, Mom," said Nick, with Grampa adding, "I'll bring him home when we're through."

Fifteen minutes later, they stepped into Mr. Weinman's shop. Although he was helping another customer, he waved and called out, "Welcome back, Nicholas."

"Good to see you again, Albert," Grampa replied.

Nick snorted impulsively, his hands flying to his mouth in an attempt to cover his impropriety. But it was hard not to laugh. In addition to the wild, light-gray hair Nick was expecting, Mr. Weinman's rather large nose, heavy mustache, and drooping eyelids did indeed give the impression of the famous Albert Einstein. Nick understood immediately why Grampa could remember to call him Albert and why Mr. Weinman so easily recalled the name Nicholas. Both names perfectly fit their owners.

Nick looked over the shop appreciatively. The room was small and narrow, and a well-lit glass display case ran its length. Despite the shop's modest size, it accommodated a vast collection of coins, many set within a cut-out circle centered in a small, white, cardboard square and held in place with thin layers of transparent film—a common type of coin holder, known variously as a *coin-flip* or a *two-by-two* (since it is two inches tall and two inches wide), that protects the coin and allows both sides to be visible. Some of the coins on display Nick recognized from the ones he had received from Grampa, such as Indian Head cents, two-cent pieces, and silver dollars. But most of them, despite being old, were new to Nick—pennies that were unusually large, a tiny silver coin labeled *"three-cent piece,"* dimes depicting Lady Liberty wearing a

cap, and many others. Grampa had been right—
What a fascinating place!

"Welcome to Weinman's Coin Shop! And who do I have the pleasure of addressing?"

Nick had been so preoccupied with the display case that he hadn't noticed the other customer's departure, nor the fact that Grampa and Mr. Weinman had been quietly chatting for a few moments. The store proprietor smiled and reached out, and they shook hands.

"Nick. I'm named after my grampa."

"A good name! And since I already know your grandfather's name," and he gave Nick a knowing wink, "that will make it easy for me to remember your name as well."

Mr. Weinman turned, took a small tray from a shelf, and placed it on top of the glass display case. "Your Grampa Nicholas tells me that you collect old wheat pennies. If you like, you can sort through these and see what you can find."

Sure enough, the tray was filled with old Lincoln cents. Mr. Weinman set a small but powerful magnifying glass next to the tray, and while the two adults continued their conversation, Nick spent the next ten minutes or so happily sifting through the little copper coins, examining dates and mintmarks through the magnifier, and setting aside the ones he was sure he didn't already own.

"I think that's it," Nick announced at last, a dozen pennies laid out on the counter, including two that he found particularly impressive— a 1911 cent (*Wow!* Nick thought. *This one's well over a hundred years old!*) and a strange 1943 cent that appeared to be gray rather than the familiar bronze.

"Looks like you have some good choices here," Mr. Weinman said, scooping up the coins and taking them to the cash register where he began writing figures on a receipt.

Nick's eyes were drawn once again to the coins in the display case, which seemed to have a strangely mesmerizing effect on him. "You sure have a lot of interesting coins here, Mister Weinman. I'd sure like to learn more about them."

Having completed his calculations, Mr. Weinman walked to another section of the shelves and pulled down a book. He set it in front of Nick. Spiral-bound with a red cover, the book was small but quite thick, and Nick opened it curiously.

Mr. Weinman tapped the book with one finger. "If you want to learn about coins, then this book is an absolute must. It will give you the history of each U.S. coin, its size and composition, and the price you might expect to pay in each of its various conditions." He glanced at Nick's grampa. "Not that I'm trying to sell you anything, but this little book will give you all the information you need about any of the coins you see here in my display case. And frankly, it's not very expensive."

"We'll take it, too!" Grampa stated emphatically.

"Thanks, Grampa!" Nick wrapped both arms around his grandfather's middle and gave him a squeeze.

"You're welcome, Nick. And is there anything else here you're interested in?"

"I don't think so," he replied. "But Mister Weinman? I do have a question for you."

"What's on your mind?" he asked, leaning toward Nick, his elbows on the glass counter.

"Well, I was looking at the pennies in the display case, and some of them, like the Indian Head pennies, I recognized because I have a few that Grampa gave me. But there are other ones, like one that had an eagle on it, that I've never seen before, and then there are some that look like pennies, but they're just way too big. So, what are they?"

Mr. Weinman was silent for a moment, and his mustache twitched, and one eyelid drooped even more than usual, a look that might have caused Nick to snicker had his question not been so serious. Finally, the store proprietor stood up straight, palms on the counter, and said, "I think the best way for me to answer your question is to give you a short history lesson on U.S. pennies, especially since your name is Nick. You'll see shortly why that is important." He looked at Grampa Nicholas. "Do you have a few minutes?"

"Absolutely!" replied Nick's grandfather.

"Well then," said Mr. Weinman with a nod and a smile, "Here we go!"

CHAPTER 4

Stories from Mr. Weinman

Story #1—The Large Cent

"THE FIRST CENTS WERE produced at the U.S. Mint in the year seventeen ninety-three. They were made of copper, twice the weight of the half-cents that were common in those days, which made them quite large, almost the diameter of a half-dollar. By the way, although we commonly call these coins '*pennies*,' technically they have always been known as '*cents*.'"

Throughout this short, opening monologue, Mr. Weinman had been opening sliding glass doors at the back of the display case. He now brought out one of the large cents and laid it on the counter. Nick gaped in awe. Marked in ink at the top of the two-by-two was the coin's date—1795. And printed at the bottom was the price of the coin—*$385. This coin is old*, he thought, *and super-expensive!*

"Go ahead and pick it up," said Mr. Weinman, "so you can see both the front and the back. Or," he added with a grin, "as we numismatists say, the *obverse* and the *reverse*."

"Wow!" (The word came naturally out of Nick's mouth sounding more like an exhalation than an exclamation.) A female face adorned the front (*or, rather, I guess I'd better call it the* obverse, Nick thought), and *ONE CENT* could be read on the back (*or* reverse).

Nick gingerly laid the coin back on the counter and looked curiously at Mr. Weinman. "New-*miss*—new-*miss*-ma—something? What's that?"

"Well, my young friend," Mr. Weinman responded, his mustache again twitching, "it's what I think you are becoming. A *numismatist* is a person who enjoys and studies coins."

Mr. Weinman picked up the two-by-two encasing the old coin and examined it with a practiced eye. "Large cents have always depicted a profile of Lady Liberty on the obverse." He returned it to the counter. "The one-cent piece went through many changes, especially in those early days. Sometimes Lady Liberty had flowing hair, sometimes braided hair; sometimes she had a cap, sometimes she wore a tiara proclaiming 'LIBERTY.'" At this comment, Mr. Weinman placed another large cent from the display case in front of Nick, this one dated 1856 and having a much more reasonable price of twenty-seven dollars. Sure enough, the word LIBERTY was emblazoned across the head shown in profile on the obverse of the coin. "I'm showing you just two variations of how Lady Liberty appeared on the large cent. There were many others, but she always adorned the coin in some fashion."

Mr. Weinman looked back and forth between the two old coins, and he continued as though he were addressing the large cents rather than Nick and Grampa.

"By the eighteen fifties, however, the U.S. Mint had encountered a problem. Prices had been rising steadily, including the price of copper. The director of the Mint complained that it now cost more than one cent to produce each of these coins. The mint was losing money with each coin struck.

"One solution was to mix other less expensive metals with the copper—that is, to make the coins of a copper alloy. Putting this idea into practice would help, but not quite enough to solve their problem. They had to come up with some other solution.

"So, they made a radical decision. They would try making one-cent pieces much, much smaller. The ultimate question, though, was—would the public accept the new smaller-sized coins?"

Story #2—The Flying Eagle Cent

Mr. Weinman scratched his head, leaving his hair in an equally unruly state, and placed another coin on the glass counter, this one labeled "1858—$26." Nick eagerly picked it up, examining both sides as the narration continued.

"So, the Mint's master engraver, Mister James Longacre, designed a small, copper-alloy 'penny' depicting an eagle in flight—the Flying Eagle cent, which you're now holding, Nick. The coins at first were limited in their production, not intended for regular circulation. These 'pattern pieces' were shown to members of Congress and other individuals in eighteen fifty-six to see if they would make a favorable impression.

"Well, once folks realized how much money the government would save with this reduction in size, plus the fact that people could now carry around in their trouser pockets, say, fifteen cents in pennies without having to wear heavy-duty suspenders to hold their pants up, they decided these small cents would be a pretty good deal. The U.S. Mint struck the Flying Eagle cents for general circulation in eighteen fifty-seven and eighteen fifty-eight, and they were indeed very popular with most people.

"But there were problems with production. The coins didn't strike well, and the dies used in the minting process kept breaking. You could say, the dies kept dying." He chuckled, his laughter high-pitched and infectious. "Anyway, Mister Longacre again came to the rescue and designed a new small cent that would become even more popular than the Flying Eagle."

Story #3—The Indian Head Cent

The next coin landed on the countertop, and Nick began to realize that he was witnessing the formation of a historical timeline of U.S. cents. He also noticed that, so far at least, as the dates on the coins became more recent, their prices were becoming less expensive—this one was marked "1862—$13."

"The new design was, of course, the so-called Indian Head cent. It is not really an Indian head at all, but rather a depiction of Liberty wearing an Indian headdress." Pausing his narration momentarily, Mr. Weinman placed another similar coin on the countertop, this one dated 1905. "If you compare these two Indian Head cents, you might notice that the eighteen sixty-two coin is of a lighter color. That is because the earlier ones, through the Civil War, were composed of an alloy of copper and nickel, whereas the later pieces were *bronze*, an alloy of copper, tin, and zinc.

"Here's where your name comes into play, Nick," said Mr. Weinman with a wink of one droopy eyelid. "During the Civil War era, people noted the lighter nickel color of these pennies, and in popular slang they became known as *'nickels,'* or *nicks* for short." He leaned heavily on the counter so as to be eye-level with Nick. "So, you see, my young friend, if you had lived during the Civil War and made a purchase at your local general store and were getting one cent back in change, it is very possible that the cashier would have handed you one of these Indian Head cents and said, 'Here's your nick, Nick.'"

Nick laughed at the personalized play on words, but Grampa looked puzzled. "Wouldn't that have been confusing?"

"How so?" Mr. Weinman countered with a grin. He obviously anticipated the question that Grampa was about to ask.

"Well, suppose some Civil War soldier had said to a friend, 'Hey, can you lend me a nickel?' How would that friend know whether he was asking for a regular, five-cent nickel or an Indian Head penny?"

"Good question," Mr. Weinman replied. "That certainly *would* have been confusing, except for the fact that during the Civil War years, there was no such thing as a five-cent nickel. That coin wouldn't appear until eighteen sixty-six. The five-cent coin of that era was called a *half dime."* Mr. Weinman removed another coin from the display case and handed it to Grampa Nicholas. Sure enough, it was a tiny, silver coin, smaller than a dime, with a picture of Liberty seated on the front, and with the words *HALF DIME* on the back. He handed it to Nick, who noted that the coin-flip was labeled *"1853—$30."* He set it down on the countertop in a line with the others, arranging them carefully in chronological order so as to keep the timeline effect intact.

Story #4—The 1909 V.D.B. Lincoln Cent

Holding another two-by-two in his hand, Mr. Weinman continued his monologue, again seeming to address the coin rather than his two guests.

"In nineteen-oh-nine, the Mint decided to try something completely unprecedented. Up until this time, the likeness of an actual human being had never appeared on a U.S. coin. Our coinage had always depicted eagles, shields, wreaths, or the face or figure of Lady Liberty," (and here he looked at Nick) "who, by the way, in case you didn't know, was not a real person, but just a way to symbolize our nation's freedoms."

Returning his attention to the small coin, Mr. Weinman continued. "That year, you see, was the one hundredth anniversary of Abraham Lincoln's birth, so in honor of our sixteenth president, Mister Victor David Brenner designed the familiar Lincoln cent.

"However, immediately after its introduction, people began complaining about it. Mister Brenner had put something on the coin that the public found unacceptable, shocking, and absolutely scandalous! People were up in arms! They were appalled and angry! They couldn't believe what a wicked thing Mister Brenner had done!" Throughout this tirade, Mr. Weinman had been waving his hands and shaking his head in a comical display of exaggerated agitation. He handed the coin-flip to Nick, and said with a grin, "See if you can find the problem."

Nick examined one side, then the other, and then repeated the process. With a shrug, he handed the coin to his grampa, who reacted in like fashion, finally placing the old penny back on the counter.

"Give up?" asked Mr. Weinman, still grinning.

"Yes!" they said together, with Grampa adding, "It's just a regular, old wheat penny. I don't see anything wrong with it at all."

Mr. Weinman slid the magnifying glass close to Nick. "Check out the reverse of the coin, down at the bottom."

Nick obliged. Focusing the lens over the lower back of the penny, three letters popped clearly into view.

"*V-D-B*." Nick handed the two-by-two and magnifier to his grampa, who verified Nick's observation.

"Must be the initials of the designer, Victor David . . . whatever his name was," Grampa said, setting the items back on the glass display case.

"Brenner," said Mr. Weinman, completing the name. "That is correct."

"But why would that be scandalous?" Grampa asked. "Don't artists usually take credit for their work?"

"Oh, there's nothing unusual about a designer adding his initials to his work," Mr. Weinman responded. "But on U.S. coins, they were always kept extremely small and put in inconspicuous places, like at Liberty's neck or in her hair, so that even if you knew where to look, they would still be hard to find." He straightened the timeline of coins, placing the Lincoln cent at the end. "The public's objection here was that the initials were so large and so conspicuously placed by themselves in plain sight. People interpreted that as shameless self-promotion, as though he were calling too much attention to himself. The Mint almost immediately reworked the dies and continued producing the Lincoln cents, but now without the offending initials."

Nick examined the coin again. "I don't think his initials look very big. They're actually quite tiny."

Mr. Weinman chuckled. "Let's say that they're *comparatively* big. Anyway, even though Mister Victor D. Brenner created the most enduring of all U.S. Mint designs, perhaps because of the public outcry against him, he never designed another regular-issue coin."

Story #5—More Lincoln Cents

Mr. Weinman pulled a wooden tray from the shelf and placed it next to the one that Nick had sorted through, which still rested on the counter. "More Lincoln cents," he declared, and as one finger stirred the pennies, first in one tray and then the other, with surprising rapidity he found several coins and laid them on the glass display top, continuing the chronological order of the timeline.

"Here's one dated nineteen eighteen," he said, "and if you look closely, you'll see the V.D.B. initials are no longer found at the bottom of the reverse. This design lasted until nineteen fifty-eight, with only one notable variation."

Mr. Weinman pointed to the next cent in line, and Nick noted immediately that it was another 1943 gray-colored penny like the one he had selected earlier.

"Why is it gray, Mister Weinman?"

"Originally, it was a shiny silver color. This cent is made of steel, coated with zinc. The war effort in nineteen forty-three had largely depleted our supply of copper, so the solution was to make these 'steel pennies.' With time and use, they turn gray, and finally almost black.

"In nineteen fifty-nine, which was fifty years after the appearance of the first Lincoln cent, the reverse was redesigned with a depiction of the Lincoln Memorial." Mr. Weinman tapped the next coin, then bent down and lowered his voice as though he were telling a secret. "Here's a riddle you can ask your friends. How many pictures of Abraham Lincoln are on a penny?" He blinked, and his mustache twitched.

"One?" Nick guessed.

"Sometimes." Mr. Weinman chuckled. "But not on this nineteen fifty-nine cent. Look carefully inside the Lincoln Memorial on the reverse."

Nick took the magnifier and did so. "It's really small," he said, squinting through the lens, "but—oh, it's the statue of Lincoln!"

"That's right," agreed Mr. Weinman. "So, at least for this coin, the answer to the riddle is not one, but two—a portrait of Lincoln on the obverse and a tiny statue of Lincoln on the reverse."

The store proprietor rummaged around underneath the cash register for a few moments and retrieved a small plastic bag containing several pennies. "Well, it seems as though every fifty years the U.S. Mint feels the need to do something different with the Lincoln cent, and sure enough, in the year two thousand nine, honoring what would have been Lincoln's two-hundredth birthday, four special reverses were struck to commemorate the four stages of his amazing life."

He dumped the contents of the tiny plastic bag onto the counter, revealing four, shiny, copper-colored coins, and then flipped several over so that the reverse of each coin was visible. "Let me get them in order," he said emphatically, sliding them into position. Nick and Grampa both leaned closer to gain a better view.

"The first in the series shows a log cabin, symbolizing Lincoln's birth and childhood. The next coin depicts Lincoln as a young man resting from his log-splitting labors and reading a book. The third reverse honors his early political career with the Illinois Capitol in the background. And finally, the unfinished U.S. Capitol building is shown as it appeared during Lincoln's presidency."

One final coin rested on the countertop, and Mr. Weinman slid it into proximity with the others. "This, my friends, finishes the history lesson. Since twenty ten, the reverse of the one-cent coin has been a shield, representing the union that Abraham Lincoln fought so hard to preserve. Can you read the motto on the shield, Nick?"

Nick leaned forward for a better look at the tiny letters. "It says, *E PLURIBUS UNUM.*" He looked first at his grandfather, then at Mr. Weinman. "I should know what that means, but I can't remember."

"Out of many, one," Grampa said reverently. "Our country is comprised of many states but remains one nation."

"So, there it is!" declared Mr. Weinman, his arms spread wide. "The history of the United States of America, at least from the perspective of the humble penny."

A smattering of applause from two pairs of hands echoed through the little room, with Grampa adding a hearty *"Bravo!"* Mr. Weinman bowed dramatically.

"That was quite a presentation," declared Grampa, "and in view of all the history here on display, I think we need to make one final purchase." Nick felt a hand on his shoulder and looked up at his grampa's whiskered face. "So, Nick, how about one last coin? Which one of these items on display would you like? Any one of . . ." Grampa paused midsentence, suddenly staring wide-eyed at the initial coin at his far left. He had forgotten about the 1795 large cent with the price tag of three hundred eighty-five dollars!

Mr. Weinman noticed the appalled expression and immediately recognized the reason for it. With a flourish like a magician's sleight of hand, he snatched the offending coin and resettled it in its former position within the display case.

They all laughed good-naturedly, and Grampa breathed a sigh of sincere relief. "Alright, then. *Now* I can say it. Any one of these coins, Nick. Which one would you like?"

Liberty Heads, Flying Eagles, Indian Heads, Lincolns, and even the half dime—Nick liked them all. How could he choose? Each one, he realized, was an actual piece of American history, and because of that, each had a story to tell. And it was all *one* story, the *American* story, *E PLURIBUS UNUM*—out of many, one, so that even if one small coin were missing, the tale would be incomplete. Nick felt as though he couldn't make a choice. But then his gaze steadied on one coin, and he smiled.

"I'll take the nick."

"Ah, perfect!" said Mr. Weinman, scooping up the 1862 Indian Head cent. He took it to the cash register and completed writing the receipt. Grampa paid the bill.

"Here you go, young man," said Mr. Weinman with another twitch of his bushy mustache. "One coin book," and he handed Nick the red, spiral-bound volume, "a dozen wheat pennies," and Nick received an envelope containing the twelve Lincoln cents he had selected, "and last but not least," the store owner concluded with an impish grin, "Here's your nick, Nick."

CHAPTER 5

Debt

THE NEXT SEVERAL WEEKS rushed along in a blur of holiday preparation and activity. Thursday, November twenty-eighth arrived with Grampa Nicholas and Uncle Rich joining the Benson family for Thanksgiving dinner. When asked what he was thankful for, Nick stated without hesitation, "The huge turkey!"

They all laughed except for Uncle Rich who looked around the table and admitted, "Okay, I'm baffled. What's so funny?"

Mr. Benson provided the answer. "Well, Rich, it's like this. Nick likes leftovers. And ever since he was little, his favorite post-Thanksgiving meal has been a dish he created himself—a cold stuffing, turkey, and cranberry sauce sandwich."

Uncle Rich turned up his nose and addressed his nephew in mock revulsion, "Yuck! Why not add some candied yams, too?"

"Oh, Uncle Rich," Nick replied in apparent sincerity, "that would be disgusting."

Nick liked his Uncle Rich, who was a bachelor and his father's older brother. Since he lived an hour away, Nick didn't see him often. Looking at his uncle and grandfather, who sat side by side at the table, Nick noted how different the two were in appearance. Uncle Rich was tall and thin, clean-shaven, with dark, brown hair. Black-framed glasses seemed a permanent fixture of his face, and he was dressed in navy slacks, brown loafers, and a white, button-down shirt, no necktie, which was for him casual attire. Compared with Grampa's flannel shirt, stocky frame, and snowy, whiskered face, the two seemed polar opposites, yet both were lots of fun to be around.

Nick had always found it amusing that Uncle Rich was a bank manager. *Of course, a person named Rich would work with money all day long*, he often thought. *Uncle Rich is rich, rich, rich*, he now sang silently in his head, *and his name sure fits his job.*

The days following Thanksgiving were filled with Christmas decorating, shopping, wrapping presents, a resumed school schedule, and Nick's consumption of a few of the aforementioned stuffing, turkey, and cranberry sauce sandwiches. Grampa dropped in from time to time to assist with the decorating as well as to help devour the remaining heaping amounts of leftover turkey, stuffing, mashed potatoes, green beans, candied yams, and pumpkin pie.

At first, all seemed "business as usual," but as time passed, Nick noticed subtle, disturbing changes in his grandfather's mood. He carried on conversations, but with a diminished jovial spirit. He smiled, but the twinkle was missing from his eyes. His step was a tad slower, and his shoulders a bit more hunched. Nick finally summoned the courage to ask, "Grampa, is anything wrong?"

He stood completely still for a few moments and looked at his grandson with an uncharacteristically somber expression before answering. "It's alright, Nick. It's nothing you need to be concerned about."

That answer, however well-intended, only served to trouble Nick's mind. *If Grampa has a problem*, he reasoned, *then it's my problem, too.* He recalled how he had cheered Grampa up after Gramma Audrey's funeral because he understood the reason for the sadness and knew how to handle it. Now, Nick was left in the dark and didn't know how to help, leaving a constant ache in his heart that was part sympathy and part frustration. Whatever the trouble was, Nick knew that it was something that he very much needed to know!

Several days after this troubling interaction with Grampa, Nick received his answer. He had just climbed into bed for the night, and Mrs. Benson sat on the edge of the bed saying her customary "goodnights." The conversation involved mainly "small talk," which in Nick's agitated frame of mind, goaded him into speaking his anxious thoughts out loud.

"Mom, what's wrong with Grampa?"

She sat in silence momentarily, apparently confused as to what she should say. "Nick . . ." And again, she hesitated. "I don't think it's anything you need to know."

Nick blurted out the thoughts that had been tormenting him for the past few days. "That's what Grampa told me, too. But, Mom, I *do* need to know! When Grampa's sad, it makes me sad. And I can't help him because I don't know what's going on. Is he . . . is he sick like Gramma was?"

Mrs. Benson reached out in alarm, touching Nick's shoulder. "Oh, no, Nick! It's not that! Grampa's not sick!" She studied his face in uneasy concern. "Is that what you've been thinking?"

Nick lowered his gaze with a barely perceptible nod.

"Oh, Nick, I'm so sorry," his mother said. "Grampa thought it best not to tell you because he didn't want you to worry about it." A determined look suddenly transformed her face. "They say, 'Ignorance is bliss.' But in this case, not knowing has only caused you to worry and imagine the worst. I can see now that it was wrong to hide it from you." She settled herself more comfortably on the bed and began her explanation.

"When your Gramma Audrey was so sick, there were lots of doctor and hospital bills to pay. There were treatments and medications that were very expensive. And then when she passed away, there were funeral and burial costs as well. Thankfully, your grandparents had insurance that paid for a large percentage of the medical bills. But there were still costs that weren't covered by insurance, and those charges have to be paid out of pocket. That is, Grampa was stuck with those remaining bills."

"Was it a lot?" Nick asked.

"Yes, Nick, it was. Just recently, your grandfather finally received the total amount that he is required to pay. And it is much, much more than he had anticipated. Your father and I would like to help, but we don't have that kind of money."

Nick was thinking very hard. "What about Uncle Rich? Can he help?"

His mother laughed humorlessly. "You always think Uncle Rich *is* rich. But he doesn't have that kind of money either. Besides," she added, "he is your father's brother, and Grampa is my dad, so they're actually not related. Grampa would never ask him for money—he would consider it an impropriety." A long pause ensued. "So, now Grampa is in debt." She looked intently at her son. "You know what *debt* is, don't you?"

"Sure. It means you owe somebody some money. So—how much does Grampa owe?"

Mrs. Benson sighed heavily. "A lot, Nick. A lot."

Now it was Nick's turn to look determined. "How much *is* a lot, Mom?"

She rose slowly and stared blankly at the wall before answering.

"Thirty thousand dollars."

CHAPTER 6

Nick and Logan Have an Idea

NICK AND HIS BEST friend Logan sat at the kitchen table sampling the first batch of Mrs. Benson's Christmas cookies. Nick had asked his friend to walk over and help him with some Math homework that had him stumped, and as always, Logan had proven himself to be a whiz at Math as well as a good teacher. Having stuffed the completed problems into a book bag, they were now (in addition to stuffing *themselves* with a fifth or sixth cookie each) taking a break, looking at the old coins Nick had received from his grandfather.

Logan held a large, silver coin between his thumb and index finger and whistled softly. "Wow! This is really old! Look at the date, Nick— eighteen eighty-four. What is it?"

"Look on the back," Nick advised.

Logan dexterously flipped the coin using just one hand so that it almost magically ended up between his thumb and middle finger. *He makes that look so easy*, Nick thought. *Is there anything he isn't good at?*

"ONE DOLLAR," Logan read, studying the coin's reverse. "So, this is a silver dollar, right?"

"Right. It's called a Morgan dollar because some guy named Morgan designed it."

A jerk of Logan's wrist brought the coin effortlessly back to its original position. (Nick shook his head slowly in amazement.) "So, how did you know that?" Logan asked. "That is, that it's called a *Morgan dollar*."

"I looked up some of these coins in my coin book. It tells everything you need to know about them."

"In-ter-est-ing." Logan stretched the word out as he gently set the silver dollar back on the table. He looked suddenly serious and changed the subject. "So, Nick, how's your grampa?"

"I think he's pretty upset."

(Nick hadn't meant to tell anyone outside the family about Grampa's financial worries, but Logan had accosted Nick on the playground at school, saying, "Okay, Nick, what's up? Something's bothering you, I can tell. What is it?"

Nick had started to reply, "It's nothing you need to know about," when he abruptly realized he was putting Logan in the same position he had been in when Grampa, then his mother, made that identical statement. He remembered the worry and frustration it had caused him and realized that he didn't want Logan to feel that way either. He couldn't keep the secret from his best friend, so he told him the whole story.)

Logan nodded, tapping his fingers on the tabletop. "*Anybody* would be upset if they owed thirty thousand dollars."

"You're right about that. And now my mom's getting upset, too, because she says if Grampa can't dig up enough money, he might end up having to sell his house. He doesn't want to because he's comfortable there, and my mom doesn't want him to have to sell it either because of all the memories she has of growing up in that house when she was little." He paused, and both boys were unusually quiet for a minute, Nick because of the frustration of not being able to help his grandfather, and Logan out of sympathy for his friend.

"So, Nick," Logan said, ending the uncomfortable spell of silence, "what about these coins? Aren't they worth something? I mean, could you maybe sell them for a lot of money, enough to get your grandfather out of debt?"

Nick looked over the small pile of coins and shook his head. "No . . . no, I don't think so . . ." He found himself staring at the Morgan dollar in front of Logan, and his eyebrows furrowed as he had a sudden thought. "But wait a minute—I just remembered something. When I got these coins for my birthday, my mom said, 'Those silver dollars are valuable. Don't spend them like dollar bills.'" He looked at Logan, then back at the Morgan dollar, then back again at his friend. "Logan, I think maybe you're on to something! Let's look up their values in the coin book and find out what they're all worth!"

It took only a minute for Nick to gather a pencil and a pad of paper, the coin book, and a small calculator, and then to drop them all hurriedly onto the table next to the pile of old coins.

"Here's what we'll do, Logan," Nick said excitedly. "I'll take each coin and write down its date and what kind of coin it is. You look it up in the book and tell me what the price is, and then I'll write it down. When we're done, we'll add it all up and see what we've got."

Logan had grabbed the little, red, spiral-bound book as Nick was giving these instructions and was already examining a page of coin prices. "I see a little problem here, Nick," he said, running an index finger across the page. "It lists a whole bunch of different prices for each coin," and he paused while scrutinizing some letters that appeared to be column headings at the top of the page, "and they look like they're different prices based on the quality of the coin."

Nick peered over Logan's shoulder and immediately understood his comment. "You're right, Logan. I completely forgot about the coin condition. There's a page toward the beginning of the book that talks about it." Logan slid the little book toward Nick, who leafed through the opening pages until he found the desired section.

"See, here it is. The letter 'G' stands for 'good.' That means the coin is worn so there's not much detail, but at least you can make out the date and words so you can identify the coin. Then there's 'VG' for 'very good,' and that condition has a little more detail." The two boys briefly studied the page until they felt they had a reasonable idea of all the coin conditions, including "F" (meaning "fine"), "VF" and "EF" ("very fine" and "extremely fine"), and so on. Logan took the book, and Nick settled himself in his chair, pencil and paper in hand. They were ready.

Nick arranged the coins, much as he had done on the evening of his birthday, beginning with pennies, then the two-cent piece, dimes, and so on, ending with the Morgan dollars.

"Let's start with this eighteen seventy-nine Indian Head penny," Nick stated. He studied the little copper coin carefully. "It's pretty worn. My guess is it's probably in good condition."

Logan leafed through the pages until he came to the section titled "Small Cents." He found the date 1879 and drew his finger across the page, stopping at the "G" column. "Fourteen dollars," he announced, while Nick, who had written "1879

Indian Head cent, good," as Logan had searched for the entry, now added its price.

"Here's the next one, Logan. Eighteen eighty-eight Indian Head penny, also good condition."

This one Logan found quickly, the entry being lower on the same page. "Five dollars and fifty cents." Nick wrote the information on the next line of his list.

The two boys continued working in this manner, finishing the Indian Head cents, the 1864 two-cent piece, and several old dimes and quarters. The half-dollars were next, and Nick called out, "Eighteen seventy-six Liberty Seated half-dollar, good condition."

Logan found the page and read, "Fifty-three dollars." He looked hopefully at Nick. "Hey, it looks like they're getting to be worth more now."

"Well, that's good," Nick replied, copying the coin's value in his ledger. "Next one—eighteen seventy-eight Liberty Seated half-dollar, good condition."

Logan drew his index finger down the column and quickly found the correct date. "Same price as the last one. Fifty-three dollars." He squinted at the numbers on the page. "Hey, Nick, are you sure it's not an eighteen seventy-eight-S half-dollar? Because *cruddy ducks*, if it is, it's worth—" He drew in his breath before finishing, "Thirty-one thousand, five hundred dollars!"

"You're kidding!" shouted Nick, unceremoniously grabbing the book from Logan's hands to see the number for himself. A quick look verified Logan's statement, and having slid the book back, Nick began to examine the half-dollar. He suddenly sprang from the chair and ran to his bedroom, almost immediately returning with his magnifying glass. He now made a meticulous and methodical inspection of the entire face of the coin, finally setting the magnifier down with a sigh. "Un-for-tun-ate-ly," he said, mimicking Logan's signature manner of speech, "there's no sign of any mintmark. This coin was definitely made in Philadelphia."

"Too bad," Logan sympathized. "I was really hopeful there for a second."

Another half-dollar and three Morgans later, the two had finished their research, with Nick's account of the information appearing as follows:

1879	Indian Head cent	good	$14
1888	Indian Head cent	good	$5.50
1889	Indian Head cent	very good	$6
1891	Indian Head cent	very good	$6
1893	Indian Head cent	very good	$6
1864	Two-cent piece	good	$21
1883	Liberty seated dime	fine	$18
1893	Barber dime	very good	$14
1898	Barber dime	very good	$11
1854	Liberty Seated quarter	fine	$43
1892	Barber quarter	very good	$16
1899	Barber quarter	good	$13
1876	Liberty Seated half-dollar	good	$53
1878	Liberty Seated half-dollar	good	$53
1895	Barber half-dollar	good	$29
1884	Morgan dollar	very fine	$46
1886	Morgan dollar	very fine	$46
1889	Morgan dollar	very fine	$46

Logan reached for the little calculator. "Read off all the numbers, and I'll add them up."

It took a few stops and restarts, but after several minutes of mathematical calculations, they finally arrived at the total value of all the coins.

Four hundred forty-six dollars and fifty cents.

With just a quick glance at the coins, Logan arrived at his verdict. "Well, four hundred forty-six dollars and fifty cents *is* a lot of money."

Nick's verdict was quicker. "But not when you need thirty thousand."

CHAPTER 7

Chubby Goose

ON SATURDAY, DECEMBER THE twenty-first, winter officially arrived. Nick and his mother were just putting the finishing touches on the last of the Christmas decorations—a red-and-green swag draped over the coffee table held in place with some candles, tiny battery-operated lights, and ceramic snowmen—when Mr. Benson bustled through the front door, having returned from running an errand, huffing and stomping his shoes on the doormat and waving his arms, for befitting the first day of winter, the weather was cold and cloudy and brisk.

"Check this out, Dad!" Nick exclaimed, pointing to the newly transformed coffee table. "Chubby goose, right?"

Mr. Benson strode shoelessly into the living room, removing his jacket along the way, and gazed favorably at the decorations. "Yes, Nick. Chubby goose indeed."

Nick turned with a cheerful glance at his mother. "Chubby goose, Mom?"

She gave her son a mock scowl. "Yes, Nick, it *certainly does* look like Christmas is nearly here," she said, refusing to be drawn into participating in the secret language shared by the two male members of the family.

"Chubby goose," as they all knew, was Nick's and his father's code phrase for "Christmas is coming soon." It was taken from an old Christmas carol, which at present was running repeatedly through Nick's brain in what has often been called an "earworm."

> *Christmas is coming, the goose is getting fat;*
> *Please put a penny in the old man's hat.*
> *If you haven't got a penny, a ha'penny will do;*
> *If you haven't got a ha'penny, then God bless you!*
> *God bless you, gentlemen, God bless you;*
> *If you haven't got a ha'penny, then God bless you!*

Nick had a sudden thought. *If Grampa is the old man in the song, then a penny in his hat wouldn't do him much good. Neither would a halfpenny for that matter.* As the song continued its unbidden rehearsal through Nick's mind, it slowly, of its own accord, changed to parody, perhaps because of Nick's preoccupation with Grampa and his thirty-thousand-dollar debt, or perhaps simply because that was the way his creative mind often worked. The transformed lyrics eventually finalized into something like the following:

Christmas is coming, the goose is getting fat;
Thirty thousand dollars goes in Grampa's hat.
If you don't have thirty thousand, a little less'll do;
If you haven't got a little less, I guess we're through!
God bless you, gentlemen, God bless you;
But I don't have that kind of money;
Neither—do—you!

Despite the excitement and anticipation of Christmas—freshly baked pies and cookies, lights and decorations, carols on the radio and Christmas movies on television, not to mention the beginning of school vacation—Nick's normally effervescent mood periodically warped into despondency as his thoughts kept returning to his grandfather's dilemma.

For the past several weeks, Grampa had been playing the part of Santa at all sorts of different venues. He had appeared at church get-togethers and private parties, at the assisted-living and nursing homes, at stores downtown, and even at the mall, where he had been booked for three consecutive days.

Nick asked his father about all these appearances. "Maybe playing Santa Claus so much will help," he said. "Does he get paid a lot for playing Santa?"

Mr. Benson set down his coffee mug and sighed. "I'm afraid not, Nick. He does get paid for some of the appearances, but not a lot. And you know how your grampa operates—usually he just does it for free."

Christmas Eve arrived with still no answer to Grampa's worries. He did his best to keep up his good spirits, and no one watching him passing out peppermint sticks to passersby at the mall or holding small children on his lap while listening to their Christmas wishes would have ever guessed he had a trouble in the world. No one, that is, except Nick and his parents, who saw through the façade with unavoidable heartache.

That evening after dinner, Grampa arrived at the Benson household, and they all traveled together to church for the traditional Christmas Eve candlelight service. An usher handed them candles and found seats for them toward the back of the sanctuary, as the large room was quickly filling to capacity.

The service began with the choir leading the congregation in singing Christmas carols—"O Little Town of Bethlehem," "It Came Upon the Midnight Clear," "Joy to the World." Nick had never been much of a singer, but because of the volume of sound resonating from hundreds of voices and echoing throughout the auditorium, he found he could sing right out and blend right in without slipping into self-consciousness.

On the stage at the front of the auditorium, a young woman made announcements, an older man said a prayer, and then the pastor rose to speak. His short sermon was titled "The Christmas Miracle." He talked about the miraculous birth of a baby who was called Immanuel, or God-With-Us, and how He had changed the course of history, and how He can still be a miracle for people today.

Nick would be the first to admit that he often daydreamed during the pastor's sermons, but on this Christmas Eve, he found himself listening intently. *That's exactly what we need*, he thought, inconspicuously glancing up at his grandfather who was seated beside him. *We need a miracle! Not the Christmas miracle—that already happened long, long ago in Bethlehem—but a Christmas miracle to get Grampa out of debt.*

The pastor, having concluded his sermon, asked everyone to stand, and the lights were turned completely off. He lit his candle—a tiny speck in the darkness—stepped down from the low platform, and with his flame, lit the ushers' candles. They in turn moved up the aisles, lighting the wicks of those closest to them. The flickering lights were passed down each row until, at last, the entire auditorium shimmered in the wavering glow. The scene reminded Nick of a cold, clear night with hundreds of brightly twinkling stars.

The final carol of the service began—"Silent Night." Nick joined all the others in singing the first few words.

Silent night, holy night,
All is calm, all is bright.

He stopped as the rest of the congregation continued their singing. *But I don't feel calm*, he thought. *I feel . . . what's the word? Agitated! That's how I feel! And for Grampa and me, all isn't very bright either. As a matter of fact, Grampa's situation seems pretty dark and gloomy.*

Quite naturally, Nick's thoughts turned into a silent prayer. After all, he was in church surrounded by candlelight and the moving strains of one of Christendom's best-loved carols. It was an environment conducive to talking with God.

Dear God, please give Grampa a miracle. You already gave us the Christmas miracle of a special baby, like the pastor said. Now we need a different kind of Christmas miracle, and even though thirty thousand dollars sounds like a ton of money to me, I guess it isn't too much for You . . . .

At that precise moment, a few, simple words sung by the choir and congregation interrupted Nick's prayer and rang clearly in his ears.

Sleep in heavenly peace,

Sleep in heavenly peace.

Instantly, Nick felt a warm, comforting glow inside, which blended seamlessly with the radiance of the candlelight all about him. He knew those final lyrics of the carol were about the baby Jesus lying in a manger, but somehow, in this moment, he had the distinct impression they were intended especially for him. *"Sleep peacefully tonight, Nick,"* the words seemed to say. *"All really is calm, and all really is bright."*

The song ended, the auditorium lights came back on, the congregation blew out their candles, the pastor gave a benediction, and people began to talk quietly and leave.

Nick realized he hadn't quite finished his prayer, so he bowed his head and whispered very softly, "Thanks, God." And noting the lateness of the hour on this Christmas Eve, he added, "Oh, and God? Chubby goose! Amen."

CHAPTER 8

A Christmas Miracle

As usual on Christmas morning, Nick rose before dawn. He dumped the contents of his stocking onto the carpeted living room floor and spent the next half hour or so opening little, wrapped packages, playing with small toys, and consuming a candy cane and a small assortment of rather luscious chocolates before his mother and father joined him, settling themselves on the floor and admiring his new treasures.

Breakfast on this special day, as was the Benson household tradition, consisted of nut roll, fruitcake, sugar cookies, and an assortment of fruit and berries with whipped cream, as well as coffee for the adults and milk for Nick.

Outside, the sun showed no sign of penetrating the heavy, gray clouds, and the harsh gusts that shook the tree branches guaranteed misery to any unfortunate pedestrian. Inside the Benson home, however, the Christmas tree lights shone cheerfully, Bing Crosby serenaded from the radio speaker, and welcome heat emanated from the furnace vents. Beautifully prepared presents tied with ribbon were opened in far less time than it had taken to wrap them. Nick especially enjoyed watching his parents open the gifts he had gotten them—for his mother, a cookie jar embellished with the words, GO AHEAD, DEAR, TAKE ALL YOU WANT, and for his dad, a huge roll of bubble wrap. "I tried to get you really useful things this year," he told them.

By midafternoon, a mountain of crumpled and crushed wrapping paper, ribbon, and torn boxes had been cleared away and taken to the garage in large garbage bags, the family was dressed, Mr. Benson was sipping a third cup of coffee, and the kitchen was warm and inviting, the air permeated with the mouth-watering aroma of onion, garlic, and roast beef.

Grampa and Uncle Rich, although having come from different directions, arrived almost simultaneously. Nick rushed to greet them at the front door, hugging his grandfather and shaking hands with his uncle. As he stood back to allow them to enter fully into the house, he was struck by how they reminded him of the Magi bearing gifts of gold, frankincense, and myrrh, except in this case, Grampa was bearing cartons of ice cream and Uncle Rich carried an enormous box of chocolates.

Nick was sorely tempted to ask his grandfather if he had experienced some sort of financial miracle, but he just wasn't sure how to go about it, or whether he should broach the subject at all. For instance, how could he possibly even bring it up? *"Hey, Grampa, you didn't happen to find thirty thousand dollars on the way over, did you?"* Or perhaps, *"By the way, have you gotten any huge checks in the mail lately?"* He decided just to keep quiet— if anything miraculous *had* happened, Grampa would be certain to mention it.

Coats, hats, and gloves were deposited in the closet, and everyone migrated to the kitchen, drawn irresistibly by the tempting smells and enhanced warmth from the oven. They milled about or stood leaning against the counter, chatting merrily and getting in each other's way every time a kitchen chore presented itself, until

Uncle Rich interrupted the flow of conversation, saying, "Oh! I almost forgot. Nick?"

Nick looked up from the apple pie on the counter that he had been admiring, and from which he had been snitching bits of the flaky crust from around its crinkled edge. "Here I am."

Uncle Rich, hands in his pockets, sauntered closer to his nephew. "Your grampa tells me you're a coin collector, so . . ." He rummaged in his left pants pocket and drew out an object hidden in his closed fist. "So, I thought you might like to have this."

He opened his hand, stretching it toward Nick, who took the gift excitedly, recognizing immediately what it was. "A silver dollar! Thanks, Uncle Rich!"

"You're very welcome."

"That's nice, Nick!" the other adults chimed in, more or less in unison.

Nick examined the shiny, silver coin. "It's an eighteen eighty-two Morgan dollar. That's one I don't already have!"

Uncle Rich nodded. "You've got the date right, anyway. Actually, it's an eighteen eighty-two-O

Morgan dollar. The letter 'O' indicates that it was made in New Orleans."

Nick studied the coin more closely, then stared confusedly at his uncle. "How do you know it's from New Orleans when there isn't any mintmark?" He held up the silver dollar so his uncle could get a better look, pointing to its date and the conspicuously empty space beneath it, devoid of an "O" or mintmark of any kind.

Uncle Rich smiled and took the large coin, flipping it to the "tails" side. "Look here," he said, indicating the bottom of the coin's reverse, "right where it says, '*ONE DOLLAR*.' Just above the '*D*' and '*O*' in the word '*DOLLAR,*' what do you see?"

He held the coin at Nick's eye level. Sure enough, there was a tiny letter "O" just where Uncle Rich said it would be.

Nick took the Morgan dollar and stared at it for quite some time. The adults had by now all resumed their animated chatter and cooking bustle, having for the moment forgotten all about the silver dollar—but Nick was still thinking about it, and thinking very hard.

The mintmark is on the back, he thought. *I didn't know that. I thought the mintmark was always on the front underneath the date. That's how it is on all my Lincoln pennies.* And the more he stared at that tiny, seemingly insignificant "O" mintmark, the more he was overcome with a strange feeling of excitement and anticipation, and a perplexing mixture of hope and anxiety.

Clutching the coin, he suddenly ran to his bedroom, unnoticed by all the others who were at the moment engrossed in dealing with an overflowing pot of boiling potatoes. Nick tossed the coin on his bed, and from his nightstand he retrieved his little bag of old coins, his magnifying glass, and the red, spiral-bound coin book. These he deposited on the bed next to the silver dollar.

Mintmarks can be on the back! Mintmarks can be on the back! he said to himself over and over as he shuffled through the pages of the book. Finding the desired page, he ran his finger down the "Good Condition" column, ending at the year 1878. "There it is," he whispered. "I have an eighteen seventy-eight Liberty Seated half-dollar that's worth fifty-three dollars. That is," and he slid his finger slightly down the column, "unless it's an eighteen seventy-eight-S half-dollar, just like Logan said he was hoping it would be, in which case it's worth . . ." He blew out a breath of air, ". . . thirty-one thousand, five hundred dollars!"

Nick opened the cloth bag and dumped its contents onto his bedspread. Shuffling through the coins, he quickly found the half-dollar in question and flipped it over. His heart skipped a beat, and he grabbed the magnifying glass and took a very, *very* careful look.

Back in the kitchen, Mr. Benson leaned over the beef roast, wiping the beads of perspiration from his forehead and checking the temperature registering on the meat thermometer. "Almost there," he announced, removing the thermometer and closing the oven door. "Maybe about five more minutes."

The others, licking their lips and nodding approval, had just resumed their conversation when, from the direction of Nick's bedroom, came a loud and chilling sound—*"Aaaaah! Aaaaah! Aaaaaaaaaah!"*

Without a second's hesitation, the adults dropped everything (including the meat thermometer, which unfortunately fell, irreparably broken, onto the floor) and rushed, one after the other, through Nick's open bedroom door.

"Nick, what is it?!" Mrs. Benson cried, her eyes wild and fearful.

Nick, still shouting hysterical and incomprehensible noises, was jumping up and down like a piston beside his bed, his magnifying glass in one hand and a silver coin in the other. As the astonished grown-ups looked on, Nick finally stopped leaping about, regained some measure of composure, and, still shaking, shouted, "Mom! Dad! We're rich! We're rich! It's a miracle! It's what I prayed for last night at church! It's a *Christmas miracle!*" As they all looked on, speechless, Nick turned and addressed his grandfather. "Grampa! You won't be in debt anymore! We're rich! We're rich!"

"What are you talking about?" his father interrupted, his panic quickly turning to irritation. "My goodness, Nick, you scared the living loonies out of us!"

"Sorry, Dad. But let me prove it to you!" He handed the coin and the magnifier, which he had been holding all this time, to his uncle, and then, in his excitement, practically threw the open coin book to his dad. He bounced to his grandfather, grabbed him about the waist, and with his heart still beating rapidly, he announced between many short breaths, "Okay. You're in charge—of the half-dollar—Uncle Rich. Mom and Dad—you can read—from the coin book together—and I'll stay here—hanging onto Grampa—so he doesn't fall over." Nick's unintentional levity lightened the mood, just a little, and he continued.

"Uncle Rich, read the date on the half-dollar."

His uncle raised the coin close to his eyes and said, "Eighteen seventy-eight."

"Right!" Nick agreed, and turning to his parents, he asked, "And what's the value of an eighteen seventy-eight Liberty Seated half-dollar in good condition?"

Mr. and Mrs. Benson examined the book, both of them tracing lines with their index fingers across the page and largely getting in each other's way. "Well, first of all," answered Nick's father, "we're looking at the right section—'*Liberty Seated Half Dollars*' is the heading."

"And here's the date, eighteen seventy-eight," Mrs. Benson said, pointing.

"I assume this column labeled '*G*' must be the prices for coins in *good* condition. Is that right, Nick?"

"Right," Nick concurred.

Both index fingers converged at the same spot, and Nick's parents said together, "Fifty-three dollars."

"Ha!" Nick shouted, in his excitement jumping up and down just as he had before; but now hanging on to Grampa, he threatened to knock him over with his wild antics instead of holding him up as promised. Grampa hugged him more firmly with a strong arm in a vain attempt to settle him down. "That's what Logan and I thought, too!" Nick continued. "But look on the back of the coin, Uncle Rich! Just like you told me a few minutes ago, look above the words '*HALF DOLLAR*' and tell us what you see!"

Again, Uncle Rich lifted the coin to gain a better view and flipped it to the "tails" side. "Yes, there's something there, but it's really small."

He brought the magnifying glass in front of the coin and peered through the lens. "Ah, there it is. It's an 'S' mintmark. This coin was struck in San Francisco."

Nick could barely contain his excitement. "Check again, Mom and Dad! It's an eighteen seventy-eight-*S* (and he greatly exaggerated the 'S') Liberty Seated half-dollar. What's it worth?"

Mr. Benson drew his index finger further down the column and stopped at the value of the 1878-S half-dollar in good condition. He stared at the figure, speechless.

Mrs. Benson pulled the book closer to better see the coin's value. She also, like her husband, simply stared in amazement for a moment, and then said, "Oh—my!"

"Well?" Uncle Rich's curiosity and impatience were getting the better of him.

"Thirty . . ." Mr. Benson coughed and gagged. He swallowed hard and tried again to speak, but the best he could manage was a hoarse, croaking whisper.   "Thirty-one-*thousand*-five-hundred dollars!"

The little group erupted in gasps and shouts of *"What?"* and *"Are you sure?"* and with Nick shouting above them all, "I told you! I told you!"

They passed the half-dollar and magnifier around the circle so everyone could take a good look. Each one of them, in turn, handled the coin gingerly by its edge as though it were a priceless artifact from an ancient king's tomb. Uncle Rich, who had known nothing about Grampa Nicholas' financial worries and the possibility of losing his home, was quickly brought up to date concerning the importance of this miraculous and valuable discovery.

Grampa bent down to address his grandson, whose arms were still wrapped around his waist. His whiskers tickled Nick's face. "But Nick," he said, "this coin is yours. I gave it to you. So, if it's worth thirty-one thousand five hundred dollars, that's your money, not mine."

Nick looked up, his vision partly clouded by the flowing, white beard. "It *is* my coin, Grampa. So, I can do whatever I want with it, right?"

"Well—I guess so," Grampa admitted.

"Okay then. What I want to do with the money is give it to you!"

Grampa was speechless, but Mrs. Benson laughed. "I guess that settles it!"

When the coin finally found its way back to Nick, Uncle Rich cleared his throat to gain everyone's attention. "Ahem! I don't want to throw a wet blanket over these joyful proceedings, but I think we all need to be aware that there is a distinct possibility that this coin could be counterfeit. It's always been common practice for unscrupulous people to take a coin and change a mintmark or date to make it appear more valuable."

The jubilation turned into an uneasy gloom.

Uncle Rich smiled. "But then again, perhaps it's not a fake. Maybe it's real after all! Who knows? But we'll need to find a coin expert who can verify whether or not it's genuine."

Nick and Grampa, still holding each other tightly, said together, as though it had been rehearsed, "Mister Weinman!"

"Oh!" exclaimed Uncle Rich as a new thought suddenly occurred to him. "I don't want to throw another wet blanket over this little party, but—the *roast beef!*"

"Oh! Oh!" cried Mrs. Benson, throwing up her arms and sprinting through the bedroom doorway. The others, although not quite as speedy, followed her to the kitchen in time to see her hastily removing a somewhat blackened piece of beef from the oven. She gave it a sad, critical look. "Well, it appears to be a little crispy around the edges, but hopefully it's still edible."

Mr. Benson shook his head and sighed. "I suspect this Christmas will always be known as 'The Day of the Christmas Coin and the Burnt Roast Beef.'"

CHAPTER 9

Mr. Weinman's Verdict

THE FOLLOWING FEW DAYS found Nick in an emotional state of absolute jitters. Grampa had phoned the coin shop the day after Christmas and was disappointed to hear a recorded message from Mr. Weinman informing callers that he would be away on Christmas break and would not reopen his shop until Monday, December thirtieth. "That's four days from now," Nick lamented, checking the wall calendar after Grampa had shared the unfortunate news. "*Four days* until we can show Mister Weinman the coin!"

The normally glorious post-Christmas break, which had always been filled with playing games, reading new books, working on jigsaw puzzles, building with interlocking blocks, and eating all sorts of holiday sweets and treats, was this year uniquely punctuated by recurring, impatient thoughts of the coin shop's closed doors, anxious looks at the coin book to check repeatedly on the half-dollar's price, and perhaps a dozen times a day peering at the precious coin, just to make sure there really was an "*S*" mintmark on its reverse, and it wasn't just some fantastic dream.

After what seemed like a short eternity (if such a thing is possible), Monday arrived. Mr. and Mrs. Benson had taken the morning off, and Nick had been in such a tizzy that he couldn't eat, eventually managing to gulp down half a glass of orange juice.

At a quarter to ten, Grampa drove up the driveway, and the Bensons bustled out the door and into his car. He backed the car onto the road, and away they headed for the coin shop!

"Hello, Nicholas! Hello, Nick!" Mr. Weinman called out from behind the glass counter as the group entered the little shop. His wavy hair and bushy mustache appeared even wilder than usual this morning. "And Nick? I assume this must be your mother and father, correct?"

Hasty introductions were made, and Mr. Weinman asked, "So, what brings you all here today? Some more old Lincoln cents perhaps?"

"Something we hope to be a bit more valuable than that," said Mr. Benson, taking the lead in answering Mr. Weinman's question. "And hopefully, we're selling and not buying today." He reached into a pocket and withdrew a white envelope, folded in half. He rather nervously unfolded it and reached inside. "Mister Weinman, we need your expertise regarding this coin." And Mr. Benson laid the old half-dollar on the counter.

The shop proprietor picked up the coin, examined the obverse, and nodded appreciatively. "A nice, old, eighteen seventy-eight Liberty Seated half-dollar," he remarked. He flipped the coin to its reverse and for just a second or two remained perfectly calm as he looked it over with a practiced eye. And then suddenly, he stiffened, and his countenance changed as his droopy eyes widened and his mustache twitched, and all the Bensons, and Grampa Nicholas, too, knew immediately what it was that Mr. Weinman had just noticed—*a tiny letter "S"!*

"Where did you find this?" he asked with a hoarse intensity that Nick and Grampa had never heard from him before.

"It belongs to Nick," Grampa began. "It's part of a little bag of coins that I gave him for his birthday. Many years ago, my grandfather gave them to me, so, counting all the time my grandfather had it, too, this coin has probably been in the family for a hundred years or so."

As Grampa finished his explanation, Mr. Weinman grabbed a jeweler's loupe from beside the cash register and held it up to his eye, examining the coin, front and back, very, very meticulously. He held the coin at an angle under a strong light, intently peering through the lens. The edge of the coin also underwent his focused scrutiny. Then, setting the tiny magnifier back on the counter, he moved to the other side of the cash register where a device resembling a microscope rested. Mr. Weinman placed the half-dollar in position at the base of the device, and after turning it on, he slid the coin slowly about, examining its highly magnified, digital image on a small screen. This process probably took no more than two minutes, but because of

Mr. Weinman's serious concentration, and especially because of his absolute silence as they all waited breathlessly, it seemed to Nick like another short eternity.

At last, Mr. Weinman flipped the switch of the coin magnifier to its off position, set the half-dollar on the countertop, and looked around at all the eager and curious faces. "Well," he began, scratching his head and mussing up his hair, which not surprisingly left him with the exact same appearance as before, "you certainly gave me a shock."

Mr. Benson said what they were all thinking. "So, then, what's your verdict, Mister Weinman? Is it real?"

Mr. Weinman smiled. "Yes, it's genuine." He looked at all the wide-eyed faces. "It seems that you have on your hands a very valuable coin."

"Are you sure?" Nick burst out. Despite four long days of hoping against hope that he would hear the words just spoken by Mr. Weinman, he still found himself momentarily unable to fathom the reality of this miraculous answer to prayer. "How can you tell?"

Mr. Weinman studied Nick's face while firmly pushing the fingers of his left hand through his unruly hair, an action that Nick assumed the coin dealer practiced often in place of using a comb or brush. "There are certain things I look for," Mr. Weinman explained, "like if there are any irregularities with the date or mintmark, or if there is evidence of tampering along the coin's edge. And you have to realize, Nick, that I've been in the coin business for many years now. I've examined literally hundreds of Liberty Seated half-dollars, and by now they're all like old friends." He picked up the coin, seemingly weighing it in his hand. "After a while, you just *know*."

"Alright, then," Mr. Benson continued after a pause. "Here's the big question you must be anticipating." He looked around the little group, and each one—Grampa, Mrs. Benson, and Nick—nodded knowingly. They all turned to Mr. Weinman and asked him, more or less together, "What's it worth?"

"That *is* the big question, isn't it?" he answered, once again scratching his head. "So far, I can tell you this. We're definitely talking five figures." Noticing Nick's puzzled expression, he smiled and added, "That means its value is in the tens of thousands of dollars." Nick whistled softly.

"You have several options if you want to sell this coin," Mr. Weinman resumed. "The easiest option is that I can buy it from you outright. However, I would require a few days to look through the pricing guides and make several phone calls to some of my associates and a few clients to get an idea of the interest they may have in such a coin." He picked it up and examined it again, flipping it from side to side. "It's an unusual coin," he mused. "It's the only example of this rare date and mintmark that I've ever seen."

"And our other options?" Mr. Benson asked.

Mr. Weinman placed the coin gently back on the counter. "Coins such as this one are often sold at auction. If bidding is intense, you could realize a substantially higher sale price. However, if the interest is not there, you could just as easily be disappointed. And keep in mind there are fees involved for the auction house, plus the fact that there will undoubtedly be a months-long waiting period before it even goes up for sale."

"Sorry to say, I think that's out of the question," Grampa interrupted nervously. "I don't think I have that much time to wait."

Nodding sympathetically, Mr. Weinman continued, "You could also sell it on commission, but the same problems exist—it could sell quickly, or it might sit for months. You just never know." He glanced at the four anxious faces. "Keep in mind that you could take this coin to different dealers and get a second and third opinion of its value. Even among experienced coin dealers, you can have slight differences of opinion regarding a coin's condition, and for a real rarity such as this one, a very small difference in grading can mean a significant change in its price." He smoothed his bushy mustache, which immediately sprang back to its initial state of unruliness. "By the way, I grade this coin's condition as fine twelve."

"*Fine twelve!*" Nick shouted, and startling all the others, he rushed to the end of the glass countertop where a copy of the same red coin book that Nick owned rested for the use of Mr. Weinman's customers. Nick opened it and furiously flipped the pages, quickly finding the now-so-very-familiar Liberty Seated Half Dollar section. "Logan and I thought it was probably in *good* condition, meaning it would be worth . . ." Nick ran his finger down a column of numbers, ". . . thirty-one thousand, five hundred dollars." He slid his finger to the right, settling on the figure in the *F-12* column. "But in fine condition, it's worth . . ." He gulped and stared in astonishment at the incredible figure. *"Forty-eight thousand dollars!"* Addressing Mr. Weinman, he asked, "How were we so far off?"

Mr. Weinman pointed to the half-dollar on the glass counter. "Pick it up, Nick, and look closely at the obverse." Nick obliged, and Mr. Weinman continued. "It *is* somewhat worn, which probably gave you and your friend the impression of being in good condition. But do you see the shield resting on the ground in front of Miss Liberty?"

"Sure," Nick replied.

"Well, in good condition, it's questionable whether you would be able to see the shield at all. Now, take a good look. What's written on the shield?"

Nick squinted and held the coin at an angle so that the light hit it just right. "It says, '*LIBERTY*.'"

"That's right. In *good* condition, '*LIBERTY*' would have been worn off completely. And even in *very good* condition, you would have had much more difficulty making out the word. So, the fact that you could read the inscription on the shield, along with other factors, allows me to grade this coin as fine."

"Wow!" Nick breathed, staring again at the amazing price listed in the coin book.

"One other thing," said Mr. Weinman. "Keep in mind that the values you see in this book are prices you might expect to *pay* for these coins. The price that I would offer you would be sub-stantially less. Coins are my business, you see, and I have to make a profit to *stay* in business." He looked at Mr. and Mrs. Benson. "Think of it as any store that buys products from a warehouse at wholesale prices and resells them at retail. You expect them to make some money on the deal, and, well, it works the same way for me."

"We understand, Mister Weinman," Mrs. Benson answered. "That only makes sense."

Mr. Weinman smiled. "So," he said, "it looks like you all have a decision to make."

The little family instinctively formed a huddle, and all were silent for a few moments until Mrs. Benson somewhat nervously asked, "Well, what do you all think?"

In an instant, Nick's tense and tentative expression changed to cheerful confidence. "Let's sell it right here!" He turned to the store proprietor and said, "I trust Mister Weinman."

"So do I," agreed Grampa.

Mr. Benson looked intently at his wife, who after a moment's hesitation, nodded enthusiastically.

"Then we're all in agreement," Nick's father announced. He reached out and shook Mr. Weinman's hand.

Nick spent the following few days in nearly constant, nagging suspense. It was impossible for Nick not to revert back to thoughts of the coin every few minutes. *What will Mister Weinman find out about the coin? How long will it take him to decide what it's worth? What will his offer be?* His agitated mind wouldn't allow him to escape these questions dozens and dozens of times a day, and even at night, he dreamed of nothing else but the coin.

Nick's grampa didn't fare much better. He called Mr. Weinman once or twice every day, asking if he had any additional news about the coin. On Wednesday, in addition to his phone call, he visited the coin shop in person just to make himself feel that he was doing *something* concerning the progress determining the coin's value, as illogical as he knew that was. Because of his visit and phone calls, Grampa Nicholas and Albert Weinman (who, being an easygoing and sociable sort who took no offense at Grampa's anxious and repeated questions) soon became quite good friends, and Grampa shared the reason for their excitement over the coin involving his financial dilemma. If the coin fetched a considerable sum of money, it could wipe out his debt. What a relief that would be after the past month's incessant worry!

Thursday, when Mr. Benson stepped through the front door after work, he was immediately accosted by his son, who bounced about and shouted, "It's time to find out about the coin, Dad! Mister Weinman called Grampa today and told him that he's ready to make an offer on the coin. He wouldn't give any details, but he said he hoped it would be good news! Dad, he's going to open up his shop at seven o'clock tonight, especially just for us!"

Dinner was hastily prepared, with "all hands on deck" in setting the table. As they ate, the excited conversation centered entirely on the topic of the 1878-S Liberty Seated half-dollar.

"Mister Weinman said he had good news."

"That means the coin must be worth a lot!"

"What do you suppose he'll offer for it?"

"Will it be enough to help Grampa?"

The table was cleared, and it was obvious from the uneaten remains left on each plate that the appetites of the Benson household had been severely diminished by the anticipation of Mr. Weinman's verdict. Dishes were hurriedly washed and dried and put away, and the family stood or paced anxiously, waiting for the time when they could head to the coin shop.

A car engine rumbled in the driveway, and moments later, Grampa burst through the door. "Are you ready, everyone? Let's go!" he called, a breathless excitement evident in his voice.

Mr. Weinman greeted them at the entrance of his shop, and after they had entered, he locked the door. They all gathered at the glass display case, Mr. Weinman behind the counter, and the others on the customer side. After passing the coin around so that everyone could take one last look, it was placed on the counter.

"Well, let's get right to it," said Mr. Weinman, nodding thoughtfully. He glanced at Nick. "As you know, the value of this coin as listed in the red book is forty-eight thousand dollars. That, of course, is the suggested *buying* price. What I will offer you for this coin, after consulting the price guides and some knowledgeable acquaintances, is considerably less, that is, the *selling* price." With an expression blending an odd combination of business and kindness, he announced, "I'm offering you thirty-seven thousand dollars."

Before anyone could say a word, he held up his hands. "Remember, the choice of what to do with this coin is yours. You won't offend me if your answer is no. You may want to get a second opinion of its worth or go some other route. However, if you choose to sell it tonight, I'll write you a check so you could visit the bank and have the money as early as tomorrow."

He had looked Nick right in the eye during the entirety of this speech, which Nick took to mean that the decision was his. After all, the 1878-S Liberty Seated half-dollar *was* solely his property. He stared at it for several seconds, thinking hard. It seemed unbelievable that this old, silver coin could be such an amazing answer to Nick's Christmas Eve prayer. *I'm looking right now at thirty-seven thousand dollars!* he thought. *To think that it started off being worth just fifty cents! But now, the big question is—What should we do with it?* Hoping to find some help in making this important decision, he looked up at his father who, with a very serious expression, was ever so slightly nodding his head up and down. Nick's eyes turned to his mother who smiled confidently.

Finally, he turned to his grandfather whose heavily whiskered face was the hardest to read. It betrayed a peculiar mix of anxious anticipation and unworthiness, coupled with a pending sense of hope lingering just beneath the surface. He looked tired but not defeated, ready perhaps to claim an unearned but most welcome victory. Most of all, though, as Nick looked into his grampa's eyes, he detected unmistakably a grandfather's absolute love for his grandson. Nick wrapped his arms around his grandfather's waist, and Grampa bent down, covering Nick's face in his snowy beard. Nick had made up his mind.

He smiled and, still within his grandfather's embrace, looked around the family circle. With four heads now nodding in agreement, he blurted out, "Okay, Mister Weinman. Let's do it!"

CHAPTER 10

A Rich Man

(One Month Later)

NICK LIFTED THE SLICE of pizza laden with mushrooms, red bell peppers, onions, and tiny meatballs and took a huge bite. "Mmmm," he murmured in rapt satisfaction. "Grampa? This is the best pizza in the history of the world!"

"Well, I don't know about that, but thank you," replied Grampa. "I tried to make it just the way you like it. You know, I used to help your gramma make pizza, so I remembered how to do it. She always made her own pizza dough, but that's beyond my abilities. I bought the dough all rolled out and ready at the grocery store."

"Nothing wrong with that," commented Mrs. Benson, and Mr. Benson added, "That's right, and I must admit that concerning this pizza,

I agree with Nick's assessment one hundred percent!"

Grampa had invited Nick and his parents to his house for a dinner-and-movie celebration party, an invitation that they had enthusiastically accepted.

There was indeed good cause for celebration. The Bensons and Nick's grampa had taken a holiday following their meeting with Mr. Weinman and took the check to Uncle Rich's bank. There they deposited thirty thousand dollars into an account for Grampa Nicholas, three thousand into a savings account for Nick, and four thousand into a checking account.

Why four thousand into a checking account? That was done at Nick's insistence, and with his parents' and grandfather's blessing, on the following Sunday he brought a check for three thousand seven hundred dollars (one-tenth of the total they had received from Mr. Weinman) to church and dropped it into the offering plate, gratefully whispering, "Thanks, God. You're the best!"

The next day, Grampa set to work to pay off all that he owed and soon thereafter received the notice that he was officially debt free! *Halleluia!*

And now, as the simple meal wound down to its contented conclusion, Grampa leaned back with a satisfied sigh. "Nick," he announced, "in honor of the incredible happenings of the past month or so, I have a gift for you, a gift that I think is both appropriate and highly deserved." He reached into his shirt pocket and pulled out a white two-by-two, which he handed to Nick.

Centered in the clear, thin, plastic covering of the two-by-two was an item that Nick recognized immediately—a Liberty Seated half-dollar. Nick read aloud the identifying information that had been printed on the corners of the coin-flip. "Eighteen seventy-eight—fine—ninety-five dollars." He slipped out of his chair and leaned against his grandfather, whose arms wrapped around him in a warm bear hug. "Thanks, Grampa."

"You're welcome, Nick. I called Mister Weinman several weeks ago and asked him if he could find a half-dollar with the same date as the one you sold." He chuckled and added,

"However, there's no letter 'S' on the back of this one!" They all laughed, and Grampa clutched Nick affectionately by the shoulders and held him at arm's length as he looked intently into his eyes. "You see, just yesterday, Mister Weinman notified me that he had found this coin, so I purchased it immediately. I wanted you to have it, Nick, to replace the one you sold so that I . . ." He paused momentarily, his eyes shimmering, and he blinked and swallowed hard. ". . . so that I could pay off my debts and keep this house." Again, he drew Nick close and whispered, "Thank you, Nick. I don't know what I would ever do without you. You're the best grandson I could ever dream of having."

"Well, Grampa," Nick replied in a serious tone, "that's what you get for being the best grampa!"

They all rose to clean the table. As they carried their plates to the kitchen sink, Grampa added, "So, Nick? Now, every time you look at the eighteen seventy-eight half-dollar, it will remind you of the Christmas coin."

After the cleanup, they migrated to the living room. "What movie will it be tonight?" Grampa asked. "You know I have a great many to choose from."

Nick was familiar with Grampa's movie collection, which consisted almost entirely of old, black-and-white films. When he was very young, Nick hadn't appreciated them. *They're old-fashioned and boring*, he had thought. But recently he had seen one starring an actor named John Wayne, which he thought was pretty good, and so at this moment he felt as excited as Grampa.

"What's your suggestion?" asked Mr. Benson.

"Well, I was thinking," said Grampa, rubbing his bushy whiskers thoughtfully, "how about one with Erroll Flynn and Olivia de Havilland? You know, with Basil Rathbone as the villain—a real swashbuckler!"

Nick shot a confused look at his grandfather. "A *wash buckler?* What's that? Someone washing buckles?"

"*SWASH*-buckler," the three adult voices chorused.

"A *swashbuckler*," Nick's father explained, "is a movie that has lots of swordplay. Thrust, parry, feint, stab, that sort of thing. Jumping off rocks and hacking away at each other, whacking and slashing and . . . ."

"Dear, we get the picture," Mrs. Benson interrupted. "I'll go make some popcorn while you three decide." As she walked to the kitchen, she turned and added, "Dad, I'm sure you have some nice Fred Astaire and Ginger Rogers musicals in your collection as well, ones with singing and dancing and romance."

"Indeed, I do, and they're also well worth watching." Grampa gave Nick a playful wink. "So, what'll it be?"

Nick didn't hesitate. "I vote for the swashbuckler!"

Forty-five minutes later, Nick sat thoroughly engrossed in the film. The swashbuckling part hadn't happened yet, but Errol Flynn had been unjustly arrested and sold into slavery and with the help of his fellow prisoners was even now plotting a daring escape.

Nick sat between his mother and grandfather on a small couch, holding a bowl of salted popcorn, which he ate automatically, his right hand moving from bowl to mouth apparently of its own accord. The couch afforded plenty of space, particularly with Nick nestled against his grampa's arm. Mr. Benson had claimed the recliner, and after having made himself comfortable, had watched the first ten minutes or so of the motion picture before dropping off to a sound sleep. Now, a low snore emanated from the direction of the recliner, which made the others stifle a laugh. "Well," Mrs. Benson whispered, "at least he watched more of the movie than usual!"

The old film turned out to be very good, in Nick's opinion. Just as his father had predicted, there was thrusting, parrying, feinting, and stabbing with flashing blades clashing and clanging until the villain was finally struck down, never again to thwart the dashing hero.

"Are you okay?" his mother asked, concerned that the scene had been too graphic and violent.

"Sure, Mom," Nick replied. "I just keep telling myself, *It's only a movie*. And besides, somehow when it's in black and white, it just doesn't seem so gory and real."

Having dispatched the villain, Errol Flynn won over the fair Olivia de Havilland, and the movie ended, happily ever after, of course.

Clicking the remote, Grampa turned off the television screen, and they all sat for a moment in the semi-darkness, the faint rumble of a snore disrupting the silence every few moments.

"Good movie, Grampa. Thanks!" Nick snuggled closer as a strong arm wrapped around his shoulder.

"Glad you liked it. That was always one of my favorites."

They sat motionless for a short while, just enjoying the moment, until Mrs. Benson interrupted the stillness. "I remember so vividly sitting in this very spot years ago when I was a child. The sofa was different then, but you and Mom would spend hours with me reading books. Do you remember that, Dad?"

Grampa nodded. "I certainly do. Those were good times." He glanced down fondly at his grandson and gave him a squeeze. "Just like now. These are good times, too."

Grampa gazed all around him, at Nick, at his daughter, at Mr. Benson, still asleep on the recliner, at the familiar furnishings of the room. He let out a contented sigh.

After a moment, he leaned down, his whiskers tickling Nick's face, and he spoke softly in Nick's ear, "Thanks for coming to my little party." He sat up straight and looked thoughtfully into his grandson's eyes. "Nick, I am a rich man."

Nick was a little startled at this unexpected comment, which immediately reminded him of the remarkable events regarding the 1878-S half-dollar. God had answered his prayer, but how had He done it? It had all begun in the year 1878 at the San Francisco Mint. Somehow, Great-Great-Grampa Bonny had acquired the coin and kept it for many, many years until he gave it to Nick's grampa. He in turn had saved it for sixty years or so before giving it to Nick. So, it had been in the family for at least a hundred years with no one realizing its value until Uncle Rich had pointed out the mintmark on a Morgan dollar, which then gave Nick the idea that perhaps an "S" mintmark might be found on the back of his Liberty Seated coin, just as Logan had hoped it might be. And sure enough, it was! God had worked it all out, beginning with events that had occurred over a hundred years before he was born! *Can God really do something that amazing?* Nick wondered. And almost immediately, the answer came to his mind—*Yeah, He's that smart!* He reflected a moment. *And He's that good, too!*

A gentle voice snapped Nick's thoughts back to reality as Grampa repeated, "Yes indeed, Nick. I am a *very* rich man."

Nick nodded knowingly. "You're right. That Christmas coin sure was worth a lot of money."

Grampa smiled and mussed up his grandson's hair. "Oh, Nick," he said warmly, "I wasn't talking about the Christmas coin."

A Note to the Reader

ALL THE COINS LISTED in this story are real, including the 1878-S Liberty Seated half-dollar, which is indeed very valuable. If you, dear reader, should ever happen upon one of these rare, silver coins, *do not spend it!* Rather, you should find a coin dealer such as Mr. Weinman, and maybe along with your five-figure transaction, you might even be treated to some more fascinating, historical stories about U.S. coins.

www.ingramcontent.com/pod-product-compliance
Lightning Source LLC
La Vergne TN
LVHW091155080426
835509LV00006B/691